BENJAMIN WHITE

FILM ANALYSIS HANDBOOK

Analysing Films, Movies and Cinema

Published in 2024 by Amba Press, Melbourne, Australia
www.ambapress.com.au

© Benjamin White 2024

All rights reserved. No part of this book may be reproduced or transmitted in any form or by any means, electronic or mechanical, including photocopying, recording or by any information storage and retrieval system, without prior permission in writing from the publisher.

Cover design: Tess McCabe
Editor: Rica Dearman

Some of the images have been generated using AI.

ISBN: 9781923116610 (pbk)
ISBN: 9781923116627 (ebk)

A catalogue record for this book is available from the National Library of Australia.

Contents

Chapter 1	Introduction to film analysis	1
Chapter 2	The language of film	9
Chapter 3	Narrative and storytelling in film	17
Chapter 4	Genre in film	25
Chapter 5	Directing and the director's vision	33
Chapter 6	Acting and performance	41
Chapter 7	Sound and music in films	47
Chapter 8	Editing and post-production	55
Chapter 9	Film criticism and analysis	63
Chapter 10	Writing an analytical essay on film	69

CHAPTER 1
Introduction to film analysis

Film, as a medium, is more than just entertainment. To some, it is an art form that combines visual storytelling, auditory elements and narrative techniques that all work together to create an immersive storytelling experience. In this chapter, we'll explore the basics of film analysis, which are the things you need to know to effectively analyse the film you're studying in your English or Media Studies class.

The evolution of cinema

To effectively study film, you need to understand where it came from, its history. So, here's a crash course. The development of cinema from the late 19th century's silent films to the modern digital, blockbusters that we so enjoy today is important in understanding the evolution of film techniques and narrative styles.

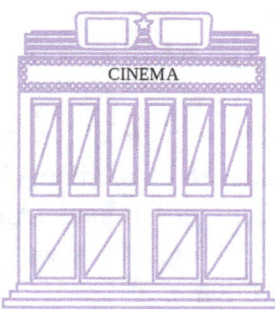

The development of film technology enabled a rapid growth of cinema into a dominant art form and mode of cultural expression. Some key developments include:

1890s
- The early, silent film era, with film pioneers like the Lumiere Brothers and Georges Melies establishing filming and projection technology, and narrative conventions.

1920s
- The introduction of sound and basic colour processes like Technicolor opened up new creative avenues in storytelling and production values.

1940s–50s
- Further refinement of colour and widescreen formats along with advances in camera technology gave rise to lavish studio productions like historical epics and musicals.

1970s
- The advent of affordable, portable cameras and easier editing processes spawned influential independent film movements like Italian Neorealism and French and British New Wave cinema. These brought fresh styles like location shooting, jump cuts and experimentation.

1980s
- The use of computer-generated images (CGI) in films like *Tron*, morphing effects in *Terminator 2: Judgment Day* and other digital innovations pushed the boundaries of visual storytelling further. Blockbuster event films became dominant.

As technology progressed, each era of filmmaking was able to bring new perspectives and ideas to the screen, challenge existing norms and develop a unique cinematic language. An understanding of these major developments and movements will help you to effectively analyse the text you're studying.

Purpose and relevance of film analysis

Beyond just understanding plot and character, analysing films involves examining the choices made by filmmakers – what styles, techniques and elements are used, and why? What is the subtext behind the events that are shown? It's like when you study a book, you need to know *how* and *why* an author wrote the words they wrote, in the way they are written.

Films are cultural products that reflect the era they were made in. They reflect societal values, attitudes, historical contexts and technological possibilities, and they also challenge conventions. By studying these at a deeper level, you can decode the language of cinema, understand how films are constructed, and how these films shape cultural perspectives. Some key analytical lenses to study films include:

- **Formalism:** Analysing the form, structure and aesthetics of films.
- **Genre studies:** Studying how films adhere to and/or bend genre conventions.
- **Auteur theory:** Viewing films through the lens of the director's style and themes.
- **Feminist criticism:** Examining films through a representation of gender.
- **Historical/social context:** Situating films within their sociopolitical contexts.

Fundamental film terms

To effectively engage in the analysis of a film, you need to have a grasp of basic film language. This includes understanding the definition and significance of terms such as shot, scene, frame, mise-en-scène, cinematography, editing, soundtrack and genre. These terms are not just jargon; they represent the fundamental elements of film construction and are essential tools for your film analysis.

Here are some film terms along with their definitions:

- **Narrative:** The narrative aspects that shape a film, including elements like story, plot points, sequencing of events, cause-and-effect logic, time management, characters and character arcs – arcs is a term used for the path that a story follows.

- **Mise-en-scène:** The arrangement of everything that appears within the camera frame – the production design, costumes, props, actors, lighting, colouring and movement.

- **Cinematography:** Includes photographic aspects like shot composition, camera angles, camera movements, lighting quality and depth of field. All of these contribute to a film's visual language.

- **Editing:** This determines the narrative pacing and continuity, and shapes audience perspectives through transitions between shots and sequencing of events. Continuity editing draws viewers into the narrative flow, while montage editing builds new associations between images.

- **Sound:** Film sound includes spoken dialogue, music, ambient sounds and periods of silence. Sound often heightens the emotional impact of visuals. Diegetic and non-diegetic sounds contribute differently towards the narrative.

- **Genre:** Genres like sci-fi, horror and documentary all have specific stylistic and narrative conventions. Analysing how a text either conforms or challenges these conventions will add to your film analysis.

The art of visual storytelling

A film's narrative unfolds rapidly via a complex relationship between dialogue, images, sounds and scenes. Unlike books, films embed meaning in every frame through visual modes like composition, colour, editing and sound design. For audiences used to passively watching films for entertainment, learning to notice these details takes some conscious effort. You need to be an active viewer of films to analyse them effectively. With patient viewing and guided study of films, across a range of genres, you can learn to appreciate films as an immersive storytelling medium.

Learning and then understanding this visual language will help you to analyse everything from a film's latent message and filmmaker intent to the impact of certain styles, equipping you with the ability to interpret films at a much richer, nuanced level.

Activity: Time capsule analysis

Objectives:

- Develop an understanding of the relationship between films and the historical/social contexts in which they are created.
- Practise identifying specific elements that reflect a particular time period.
- Use critical thinking about how films shape and are shaped by societal values.

Instructions:

1. **Film selection:** Choose a film that is set in a particular historical period or clearly explores themes linked to a specific era or social movement.

    a. Historical time period: A film set during the First or Second World War, the Great Depression or the Victorian era.

    b. Social movements: A film about feminism, environmental activism, LGBTIQA+ rights or exploring social justice issues.

2. **Viewing:** Watch the film with the specific goal of identifying elements that reflect its time period or the social context it explores. Take notes on:

    a. Costumes, hairstyles, set design, props and the technology that is visible

    b. Slang, accents, specific vocabulary and formal versus informal speech

    c. Consider the music of the time – popular genres or iconic songs

    d. The portrayal of relationships, power dynamics, social norms and customs

3. **Analysis and discussion:**
    a. What specific elements in the film helped you to identify its historical/social setting?
    b. How do the values, attitudes and social dynamics portrayed in the film differ from or reflect our contemporary society?
    c. Do you think the film could have been made in a different time period? Why or why not?
    d. How does the film's setting/context contribute to the overall themes or messages explored?
    e. Can you think of any modern films that deal with similar themes or social issues? How do the portrayals compare?

Extension:

- Analyse two films set in different historical periods or that explore different social movements. Examine how these contexts shaped the filmmaking styles and the messages conveyed.
- Reimagine a scene from the film you watched and update it to reflect contemporary society. What elements would need to change? What would stay the same?

CHAPTER 2

The language of film

In the world of film, storytelling relies heavily on more than just spoken language. In this chapter, we will explore how filmmakers use visual elements to narrate a story, create a mood and develop characters.

Composition and framing: The art of the image

Every shot in a film is carefully composed. Composition refers to the arrangement of visual elements with the frame. This includes the positioning of the characters, the placement of objects and the use of space. Framing, on the other hand, involves how these elements are enclosed within the borders of the frame. Together, composition and framing guide the audience's attention and convey subtextual information beyond the script.

Here are some concepts of composition and framing:

- **Rule of thirds:** Dividing the frame into horizontal and vertical thirds helps place important elements along these lines or intersections for optimal focus.
- **Negative space:** The empty space around and between subjects. Managing negative space balances busy and sparse areas for best composition.
- **Leading lines:** Diagonal lines, roads, fences that direct the viewer's gaze towards important subjects.

- **Symmetry versus asymmetry:** Symmetrical framing conveys harmony while asymmetry creates visual tension.
- **Off-centre framing:** Positioning subjects slightly away from the centre makes the scene subtly tense.

Framing refers to how tight or loose the camera shot is – how much background area versus the main subject is visible within the frame borders. Tighter framing tends to focus attention more narrowly versus loose framing, which provides more context. Manipulating composition and framing together helps to emphasise visual details that help carry the film's non-verbal messaging.

Colour theory

The colour of a film is not an accident. Directors use colour psychology to manipulate our emotional responses to their films. Warm colours like red, yellow and skin tones evoke intensity, energy and optimism, while cool colours like blue and grey can indicate gloom and fear. Here, we explore how different colours can represent various themes and moods, and how colour palettes are chosen to complement a film's overall tone.

The Matrix uses a sickly green filter to indicate the disturbing simulated reality of the Matrix.

In *Spider-Man: No Way Home*, red and blue colour-code the two universes from which the protagonists enter.

High-contrast black and white in *Mad Max: Fury Road* enhances the film's stark, post-apocalyptic look.

Colour is used in films in the following ways:

- **Warm versus cool colours:** The emotional impact of different colour temperatures.
- **Colour motifs:** Recurring colours can symbolise different themes and ideas.
- **Colour and genre:** Some colour schemes are genre specific.

Lighting: Setting the tone

Lighting in film is essential for creating atmosphere and depth. It can be used to enhance emotions, create tension or focus attention. Here are some key lighting techniques and their effects on storytelling:

- **High-key lighting:** Minimises shadows through diffused, uniform lighting as often seen in cheerful comedies and musicals.
- **Low-key lighting:** Creates a dramatic effect with strong contrasts using little key lighting on subjects against dark backgrounds. *The Dark Knight* trilogy uses this to build gritty intensity.
- **Backlighting and silhouetting:** Separates subjects in the frame for depth and visual interest. The ring of light around characters isolates them and builds mystery.
- **Practical lights:** How onscreen light sources impact a scene.

Cinematography: The moving image

A film's visual language profoundly impacts the storytelling and the audience's experience. Creative filming choices combine camera shots, angles and movements in clever ways to build emotion and add to the dramatic tension of the film.

Here are some basics:

- **Shot sizes:** These play with the camera's distance from the subject. Extreme close-ups magnify intimate details provoking strong audience reactions; long shots illustrate backgrounds adding context, allowing the audience to process the broader landscape.
- **Camera angles:** Angles leverage the audience's perspective. Low angles make powerful impositions, while high angles convey vulnerability. Eye-level angles bring neutrality.
- **Camera movements:** Panning, tilting, tracking and their narrative implications.

Making movies relies on a lot of camera trickery. The table below shows some of the common shots, angles and camera movements that directors employ to pull the audience into the storytelling. There are many more techniques, but these are the most common you'll come across in your film study.

Shot sizes	Camera angles	Camera movements
• Extreme close-up: Intensifies emotions	• Low angle: Powerful perspective	• Tracking: Builds tension following subject
• Close-up shot: Focuses on reactions	• High angle: Vulnerable perspective	• Tilt: Vertically reorients perspective
• Medium shot: Personal framing	• Eye level: Neutral perspective	• Pan: Horizontally establishes setting
• Mid-long shot: Includes interactions	• Bird's-eye view: Reveals geography	• Crane: High angle overview
• Long shot: Establishes background	• Canted angle: Disorients	• Handheld: Immediate, raw
• Extreme long shot: Illustrates scope	• Overhead angle: Confinement	• Zoom: Rapidly maginifies focus

The role of mise-en-scène

Mise-en-scène refers to everything visible within the camera frame that contributes to the overall look, feel and meaning of a scene. It combines production design elements like sets, props, costumes and cinematographic choices of lighting and blocking to build an immersive storytelling moment.

Here are some examples of what you'll find within mise-en-scène:

- **Set design and props:** The production design team conceptualises every set built and prop placed on these sets. Nothing is left to chance. Sets and props are built to reinforce the narrative arc at each point.

- **Costuming and make-up:** Costume designers collaborate closely with the director and producer, carefully studying character profiles and scenes. They do this so they can select silhouettes, textures, colours and accessories that underline the personalities of the characters being portrayed.

- **Blocking and staging:** Blocking refers to the precise choreography of the actors in the scene – where and how they stand, sit, enter and exit the frame. Staging adjusts scene objects and lighting to complement blocking and the scene's dynamics.

Activity: Scene analysis

Objectives:

- Practise identifying and analysing key film elements within a chosen scene.
- Understand how these elements contribute to the overall meaning and effect of the scene.

Instructions:

1. **Scene selection:** Select a short scene from a film. You can find many on YouTube – choose one from your favourite film.
2. **Viewing:** Watch the scene once without taking any notes, just let it play out.
3. **Repeat viewing:** Watch the scene again. This time, take note of some of the things that are mentioned in this chapter:
    a. Mise-en-scène
    b. Cinematography
    c. Editing
    d. Sound
4. **Analysis and discussion:** Consider how these elements work together in the scene to convey meaning.
    a. What is the overall mood or tone of the scene?
    b. How do the visual and auditory techniques contribute to this?
    c. Does the scene adhere to genre conventions or challenge them?

Extension:

- Compare different scenes side by side to examine how film techniques change the audience's experience.
- Take a screenshot of a scene and analyse it as if it was a photograph.
- Research the historical and social context around the time the film was made and consider how that might have impacted the choices made in the scene.

CHAPTER 3

Narrative and storytelling in film

Narrative structure in film is the backbone of storytelling. It's the framework that guides us through the cinematic journey, shaping our experiences and our emotional response. Understanding the narrative structure of the film you're studying is not just about following its plot; it's about comprehending the art of storytelling and how filmmakers weave complex tales. This chapter will guide you through some of the elements that make up the narrative and storytelling in films.

The three-act structure

The three-act structure is the foundational narrative model in cinema, providing a clear and effective framework for storytelling. This structure divides the narrative into three distinct parts: set-up, confrontation and resolution. Here's how the story unfolds over three interconnected stages:

1. **Set-up:** Introduces the protagonists, their status quo lives and the thing that spurs them into action. In *The Matrix*, Thomas Anderson's mysterious encounters with cryptic messages set up the technological conspiracy he uncovers as Neo later in the film.
2. **Confrontation:** Focuses on the escalating tensions, obstacles, inner doubts and learnings encountered in the protagonist's

pursuit of their goal. Staying in *The Matrix*: Neo must come to terms with the simulated reality of the Matrix and his own powers. Subplots like romance, great action sequences and important reveals often occur to hold our attention.

3. **Resolution:** The climax of the film arrives when the loose ends get tied up, character arcs achieve closure and the core conflict gets resolved in an emotionally satisfying way. Neo embraces his role as 'the One', defeats Agent Smith and awakens others trapped in the Matrix with his greater understanding.

> Films like *Star Wars* and *The Godfather* exemplify the three-act structure, using it to build their narratives effectively.

Alternative structures

Beyond the traditional three-act format, filmmakers sometimes apply alternative narrative structures to their stories. These include non-linear storytelling, where events are presented out of chronological order; the use of flashbacks to provide background or context; and parallel narratives that weave together multiple storylines.

Movies like *Pulp Fiction* and *Memento* use non-linear structures to great effect, creating complex, engaging narratives. These alternative structures can challenge viewers, requiring them to actively piece the story together. These structures also offer fresh and innovative ways to tell stories on the big screen.

> Flashbacks reveal backstories, which build emotional connections to the current events being shown. In *Titanic*, elderly Rose reminisces about her fateful romance with Jack, set decades in the past.

Character development and character arcs

Characters are at the core of any film. Their development is essential in driving the story forward – a film would be pretty dull if a character didn't do anything or learn anything, wouldn't it? Central to this is the protagonist's character arc, which traces their inner journey and transformation throughout the film. Well-developed and well-rounded protagonists are key in crafting an engaging and compelling narrative.

The protagonist usually undergoes a character arc that aligns with the film's three-act structure. In the first act, we are introduced to the protagonist's world and their flaws. The inciting incident at the end of the first act sets them out on a journey of change. In the second act, the protagonist encounters tests and trials that challenge their beliefs and way of thinking. This builds to the climax and resolution of the third act, where the protagonist undergoes a major transformation and can resolve their inner conflict.

Act 1   **Act 2**   **Act 3**

In addition to the protagonist, supporting characters and antagonists provide sources of conflict, act as mentors, add comedic relief or mirror the protagonist, adding layers of complexity to the narrative. Interesting supporting characters who undergo their own character arc add richness and depth to the film. Finally, a complex and dynamic antagonist – 'the baddie' – who contrasts and parallels the protagonist, can lift the stakes and add to the tension of the film.

Themes and symbolism

Themes are the core underlying messages that a film aims to explore. Well-constructed films use the narrative arc and cinematic elements to explore its central themes in a meaningful way. Themes may be complex philosophical concepts or universal ideas that speak to our shared humanity.

Symbols and motifs are objects, visuals, sounds, colours, numbers or events that repeatedly appear throughout the film and reinforce thematic concepts. For example, trains appearing throughout a film may symbolise the protagonist's desire for freedom or escape. The recurrence of the colour red may signify danger, passion or violence connected to the film's themes.

Analysing how themes develop and evolve over the course of the film you're studying will help you to reveal the text's deeper layers of meaning. Exploring which symbols or motifs accompany major narrative turning points or character arcs can provide insight into how the filmmaker has woven together the story and theme.

Pacing and timing

Pacing and timing are crucial elements in narrative structure and storytelling. We've all sat through a film that felt like it went for aaaaaages. Nothing happened. It was boring. Effective pacing ensures that the narrative maintains a rhythm that keeps the audience engaged, building tension and emphasising key moments.

For instance, the deliberate pacing of *Gravity* heightens the suspense and claustrophobia of the space setting. Filmmakers use pacing as a tool to control our emotional journey, guiding us through the narrative's highs and lows.

Writing about narrative structure

When writing about narrative structure, it's important to use specific examples from the text you're studying to illustrate your points. Here are some practical tips for your essay:

- Outline the key elements of narrative structure – exposition, inciting incident, rising action, climax, falling action and resolution – then identify and discuss how specific scenes in the film align with each element. How do these moments contribute to the overall story?

- Pinpoint key turning points in the plot and examine how they drive the protagonist's character arc and how they transform from beginning to end. What is the protagonist's flaw in the beginning, and how does their change manifest in climactic moments?

- Analyse how the film's themes and central ideas develop and build across the three acts. Discuss how the climax delivers the thematic message. Observe how symbols and motifs emerge across the structure to reinforce these themes.

- Unpack how supporting characters influence or catalyse the protagonist's transformation and link this to their interactions at various narrative stages. Examine character foils and relationships.

- Note any patterns, repetitions and contrasts between different parts of the structure – how do symbols, colours, objects or contrasts reinforce key ideas?

These sentence stems will get you started with analysing the narrative structure of your text:

1. As the exposition unfolds in scenes such as [scenes], the viewer gains insight into the protagonist's worldview and their core weaknesses, including [details from film], foreshadowing their transformation to come.

2. The inciting incident introduces the central conflict when [explain event], forcing the protagonist into an uncomfortable confrontation with [explain impact on protagonist] that ultimately launches them on their journey.

3. Over the course of the second act, themes of [theme] emerge through moments such as when [example] conveys [describe how it develops chosen theme], deepening this idea that later comes to a head at the end of the film.

4. The turning point in the narrative arrives when [describe event], representing the emotional peak of the protagonist's arc as they finally [explain how it transforms them].

5. Ultimately, the end of the third act depicts the protagonist [describe how they have changed], demonstrating they have overcome [explain original flaw], completing their narrative transformation from beginning to end.

Activity: Scene dissection

Objectives:

- Develop an understanding of how individual scenes contribute to the overall narrative of a film.
- Analyse the pacing and rhythm within scenes and across the film.

Instructions:

1. **Scene selection:** Select a pivotal scene from the film you're studying that demonstrates a shift in tension, character development or thematic exploration. Ideally, pick a scene that runs for about seven minutes.
2. **Analysis and discussion:** Break down the scene, considering the following things:
    a. Three-act placement: Where does this scene fall within the film's three-act structure?
    b. Pacing: Divide the scene into smaller segments (they could be by camera shot, dialogue, etc.). Analyse how pacing shifts throughout the scene. Are there slow moments, bursts of action or moments of pause?
    c. Visuals: How do camera angles, shot composition and lighting contribute to the mood and pacing of each segment?
    d. Sound: How does music, sound effects and dialogue influence pacing and build tension in each segment?
    e. Narrative impact: What is the purpose of this scene within the larger narrative? How does it drive the plot or character arcs forward?

3. **Scene breakdown template:**

Scene segment	Pacing (fast/slow/varied)	Visual elements	Sound elements	Narrative impact

Segment 1

Segment 2

4. **Analysis and discussion:**

    a. How does a detailed analysis of a single scene enhance the understanding of the film's overall narrative?

    b. How malleable is pacing? What specific techniques create different emotional effects?

Extension:

♦ If you have access to editing software, consider rearranging the scene and experimenting with speed and pacing, changing sequences and character development.

CHAPTER 4

Genre in film

Genres are categories that help define a film's style, tone and narrative elements. They provide a framework for both filmmakers and audiences to understand and communicate the type of film being made or watched. Genres can range from action and adventure to drama, romance, comedy, horror and beyond. Understanding the genre of your text is important for analysing it. Your task may call for you to explore how your text fits or challenges its genre. This chapter explores various film genres, their conventions and how they influence the narrative and production of a film.

Defining different film genres

Each genre has distinct characteristics that set it apart:

Action/adventure: Defined by excitement, physical challenges and a fast-paced plot.

Comedy: Focused on humour, often through situations and dialogue.

 **Drama:** Centres on emotional and relational development of realistic characters.

Horror: Aims to create feelings of dread, fear and shock.

 **Science fiction/fantasy:** Deals with imaginative and futuristic concepts. Sometimes explores the reality of the world today.

Romance: Revolves around romantic relationships between characters.

 **Thriller/mystery:** Known for suspense, tension and anticipation.

Genre conventions and tropes

Each genre comes with a set of conventions or 'tropes' – standard elements that are expected within a particular genre. For instance, action films often feature car chases and fight scenes, while horror films contain jump scares often in an isolated setting. These conventions provide a familiar structure within which filmmakers can work, but they also offer a chance for innovation. When a film plays with or subverts these conventions, it can lead to fresh and engaging storytelling. While viewing your text, you might use this list below to position it in one or more genres:

Action films	• High-stakes scenarios, physical confrontations involving elaborate choreography and stunt work, car chases and heroic protagonists overcoming incredible odds are quintessential tropes. • Locations often switch rapidly, adding to the dynamic nature of the plot. • Action films also use high-stakes dilemmas like saving the world, hostages or a loved one's life. • Watch: *Die Hard*; *Terminator 2: Judgment Day*; *Mad Max: Fury Road*.
Romantic comedies	• The 'meet-cute' scenario where the protagonists encounter each other in an amusing way, the presence of misunderstandings or obstacles to the relationship and a happy resolution are typical tropes. • Romcoms also feature a supporting cast of humorous friends/family who support the central relationship. • There are often lavish dates or outings to strengthen the romance along with moments showcasing charming chemistry between the leads. • Witty, fast-paced dialogue is also a common element. • Watch: *When Harry Met Sally*; *Pretty Woman*; *Clueless*.

Dramas
- Character-driven stories focusing on emotional and relational conflicts.
- Themes might include family dynamics, love, betrayal and personal growth.
- Well-developed characters are central to dramas, as are heartfelt conversations and emotional climaxes.
- Thoughtful cinematography and lighting often set a sombre, nostalgic tone.
- Watch: *Citizen Kane*; *12 Angry Men*; *Moonlight*.

Horror films
- Reliance of jump scares, eerie music, dark or isolated settings (haunted houses, dark forests), and the presence of supernatural entities or deranged antagonists are common.
- The narrative often revolves around survival. Horror also relies on gore, violence and disturbing imagery as well as ominous musical cues and sound effects.
- These films build tension slowly through jump scares or psychological manipulation, often exploring societal fears like disease or technology gone wrong.
- Watch: *Psycho*; *The Exorcist*; *Get Out*.

Science fiction
- Advanced technology, space or time travel, dystopian futures and encounters with alien life are often central concerns.
- These films frequently explore the impact of technology on humanity. They also provide commentary on moral dilemmas raised by technological advances.
- Slick, futuristic production design and gadgets are used alongside creative alien creature designs and planets.
- Epic space battles between spaceships are also common science fiction tropes.
- Watch: *Blade Runner*; *Star Wars*; *Star Trek*; *Alien*; *Back to the Future*.

Thrillers/mysteries
- Central mysteries or puzzles to be solved, suspenseful scenarios, plot twists that shock or surprise audiences and clever detective work are key components.
- Mysteries build intrigue through red herring and partial reveals that keep the audience guessing.
- Thrillers rely on tense music, dangerous scenarios, high stakes and a twisting, fast-paced plot to create suspense.
- Both make use of shadowy lighting and camera angles to create mood.
- Watch: *Rear Window*; *The Silence of the Lambs*; *Se7en*.

Genre blending and innovation

Filmmaking is an art form that constantly evolves, and this includes the blending of genres. Films can straddle multiple genres, combining elements of each to create a unique viewing experience. For example, a romantic comedy might incorporate elements of drama, or a science fiction film might include elements of a thriller. This genre blending allows for innovative and fresh storytelling, and can lead to the creation of a range of new subgenres.

The cultural and historical impact of genres

Genres are influenced by cultural and historical contexts, and in turn, they can reflect or shape society's attitudes. The popularity of superhero films in the past few years speaks to contemporary interests and values. Similarly, the evolution of the horror genre reflects changing societal fears and anxieties.

Genre-specific analysis techniques

Analysing a film within the context of its genre is important for a film analysis essay. This involves looking closely at how the film adheres to or challenges the typical conventions of its genre. For example, in a mystery film, one might analyse how the plot maintains suspense and intrigue, while in a comedy, the focus might be on the timing and the delivery of the humour and the jokes. Here are some more tools and techniques for analysing films in different genres:

Action/adventure

- Examine the choreography and execution of action scenes.
- Analyse the depiction of the hero archetype and their journey.
- Consider how the film uses pacing and editing to enhance action scenes.
- Look at the use of special effects and their contribution to the overall impact of the film.

Horror

- Focus on how the film creates and maintains a sense of fear.
- Assess the use of sound design, including music and sound effects, in building tension.
- Analyse the portrayal of antagonists and supernatural elements.
- Evaluate the use of lighting and camera angles to create a sense of dread.

Comedy

- Study the timing and delivery of jokes and humorous situations.
- Look at the use of irony, satire or slapstick and their effectiveness.
- Consider character interactions and their contribution to humour.
- Analyse how the film balances comedic elements with the narrative.

Drama

- Examine character development and emotional depth.
- Focus on dialogue and its role in revealing character and advancing the plot.
- Analyse the use of conflict and resolution.
- Consider the film's thematic depth and its exploration of the human condition.

Science fiction

- Analyse the creation and consistency of the film's world-building.
- Examine how the film incorporates futuristic or fantastical elements.
- Consider the themes and how they relate to current social, ethical or technological issues.
- Evaluate the use of visual effects and their integration into the story.

Romance

- Focus on the development of the romantic relationship and its authenticity.
- Analyse how the conflict is introduced and resolved within the narrative.
- Consider the portrayal of chemistry between characters.
- Evaluate the use of common romantic tropes and their execution.

Thriller/mystery

- Analyse how the film maintains suspense and intrigue.
- Examine the use of clues, red herrings and plot twists.
- Consider the portrayal of the detective or protagonist's investigative process.
- Evaluate the resolution of the mystery and its impact on the overall story.

Activity: Genre detective

Objectives:

- Develop an understanding of film genre conventions and tropes.
- Practise identifying genre elements within a film.
- Consider how genre conventions are used, subverted or blended to create meaning.

Instructions:

1. **Viewing:** Watch a film clip; it can be the film you're studying or another film of your choice.

2. **Repeat viewing:** Watch the film clip again, this time taking note of the following:

    a. Possible genres: List two to three genres this clip *might* fit into based on your observations.

    b. Evidence: For each genre you've listed, find specific examples from the clip that support your placement. This could include:
      i. Setting and visuals
      ii. Character types
      iii. Music/sound
      iv. Plot elements
      v. Overall mood/tone

3. **Analysis and discussion:** How does a good understanding of a film's genre help analyse it more deeply?

Extension:

- Compare two clips from different genres. How does an understanding of genre conventions highlight their differences?

CHAPTER 5

Directing and the director's vision

The director is often seen as the creative vision behind the film, transforming a script into a visual and auditory experience. Their role encompasses the overall artistic and technical direction of the film. Directors make important decisions about casting, performance styles, visual aesthetics and the pacing of the narrative. In this chapter, we will explore the role of the director and how their vision shapes the film's final presentation.

Directorial styles and techniques

Directors use various styles and techniques to bring their vision to life. Some focus on intricate visual compositions, while others prioritise narrative pacing or the performances of the actors. For example, the use of long takes and minimal editing can create a sense of realism, as seen in the works of Alfonso Cuarón (if you haven't already, watch *Children of Men*. Great film!). Directors like Wes Anderson are known for their symmetrical compositions and vibrant use of colour.

Case study: Famous directors and their styles

Director	Style and techniques	Representative films
Alfred Hitchcock	Suspense through camera angles, lighting, editing; motifs like staircases, voyeurism.	*Rear Window*; *Psycho*; *Vertigo*
Stanley Kubrick	Meticulous symmetry in framing, elegant tracking shots, atmospheric world-building.	*2001: A Space Odyssey*; *The Shining*; *A Clockwork Orange*
Greta Gerwig	Naturalistic acting, fresh take on coming-of-age and female perspectives.	*Lady Bird*; *Little Women*; *Barbie*
Quentin Tarantino	Clever dialogues, non-linear storytelling, homages to genre cinema.	*Pulp Fiction*; *Kill Bill*; *Once Upon a Time in Hollywood*
Sofia Coppola	Visual style focused on atmosphere, subtle performances, ennui and alienation.	*Lost in Translation*; *Marie Antoinette*
Christopher Nolan	High-concept narratives about memory/time/dreams, precise editing and pacing.	*Inception*; *Memento*; *Interstellar*
David Fincher	Dark themes, vivid colour palettes, smooth camera glides to build tension.	*Fight Club*; *The Social Network*; *Gone Girl*

Auteur theory

The auteur theory suggests that a director's personal vision and creative style are so distinctive that they become the 'author' of the film. This theory has been the subject of much debate in film criticism, as it emphasises the director's role over other contributors. Some argue that it diminishes the vital creative roles of writers, cinematographers, editors and actors. However, defenders of the theory view the director as the ultimate synthesiser of these elements. Overall, the auteur theory debate centres on the extent of the director's influence over the final form and voice of the film.

Directors like Alfred Hitchcock and Quentin Tarantino are often cited as examples of auteurs, as their films consistently reflect their unique style and thematic preoccupations regardless of other contributors. However, both have benefitted from fruitful collaborations with writers, actors and cinematographers even while imparting their distinctive vision.

The director's influence

A director's creative vision permeates every phase of bringing the film to life. During pre-production, they lead decisions on casting, location scouting, storyboards and the film's visual aesthetic. For casting, the director oversees auditions to determine which actors best embody characters while possessing the necessary acting chops. Location scouting is guided by the settings established in the script, but directors decide on places that strategically enhance desired themes and moods. Some countries and states also offer generous incentives to entice films to shoot there. Storyboarding allows directors to plan out key shots and sequences, reflecting their vision.

During post-production, directors work closely with editors on issues such as pacing, transitions and sound mixing to refine the narrative rhythm and audio landscape of the film. They may also oversee visual effects shots. Sometimes, they organise reshoots or additional shoots to fill gaps, or add to the film. Fun fact: After Peter Jackson's *The Lord of the Rings: The Return of the King* had swept the 2004 Oscars, and prior to the extended edition coming out, Jackson filmed one more scene. He had won the Oscar, yet the film wasn't 100% complete.

The director shepherds the film through each step of production, acting as the chief creative decision-maker to ultimately render their ambitions for the script onto the screen. Their influence can be felt in every frame, through to the final cut.

Analysing the director's style and vision

To analyse a director's choices, focus on how different elements are used to create a cohesive film. Look at the casting decisions, the performances of the actors, and the director's approach to pacing and scene composition. How do these choices serve the story and themes?

When analysing a director's contribution to a film, here are some key aspects to consider:

- **Shot composition:** Analyse framing, camera angles, movement and lens types to see how they convey specific ideas/emotions and shape perspective. How are shots sequenced through editing to build scenes?

- **Performances:** Look at how the director influences acting styles – are they natural, subtle or exaggerated/theatrical? How are actors moving through scenes and interacting to reveal power dynamics? Consider viewing the special features of your movie, behind the scenes or director commentary. For example, Jackson's *The Lord of the Rings* trilogy, the extended editions, have a wealth of resources included which discuss these elements.

- **Pacing and structure:** Analyse the rhythm created through editing cuts, devices like slow motion and narrative structure. How do directing choices control the flow of information and the audience's experience?

- **Visual details:** Note down specific details that embellish the world of the film through set design, props, effects, location and wardrobe, and their significance.

- **Audio:** Consider music cues, ambient sounds and dialogue – how does the audio build mood and tension? Pay attention to the moments of muted or absent sound.

When writing about a film, use specific examples to illustrate the director's style and their intent. Analyse particular scenes, dialogues or technical choices, and discuss how they contribute to the overall vision and meaning of the film. Consider the film's reception and critical interpretations, which can offer additional perspectives on the director's work. Compare different films by the same director to better understand their evolving style and thematic concerns.

Need some help to get started with your writing? Here are some sentence starters for you:

1. The director's use of [specific camera technique] in this film enhances the storytelling by...

2. Through the lens of [director's name], the recurring theme of [theme] is explored through...

3. The choice of [specific element] by the director contributes to the overall mood of the film, particularly in the way...

4. In [film title], the director's distinctive approach to [aspect] is evident when...

5. The film's [pacing, sound design, etc.] reflect the director's intent to [create suspense, evoke nostalgia], especially during...

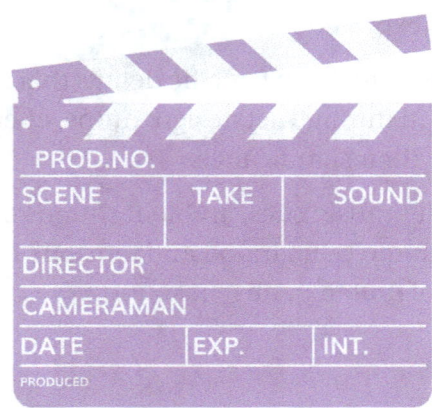

Activity: The director's toolkit

Objective:

- Understand how directors employ various cinematic tools to shape their film.
- Identify a director's recurring techniques and their impact on the viewing experience.
- Develop the ability to analyse a film on a deeper level, beyond just plot and dialogue.

Instructions:

1. **Background:** Review the information on the directors explored in this chapter. Choose one and then find two or three clips from some of their films; make sure they're from different films.
2. **Viewing:** Play the first clip. Note down any stylistic choices that seem deliberate (odd camera angles, colour choices, etc.).
3. **Repeat viewing:** Watch the clip again and while you're watching note down specific choices the director makes. Consider things like:
   a. Camera work: Angles, movements, shot types (close-up, long shot, etc.)
   b. Editing: Pace (fast cuts, slow fades) transitions (how scenes shift)
   c. Sound: Music, sound effects, notable use of silence
   d. Mise-en-scène: setting, costume, lighting, anything within the frame
4. **Analysis and discussion:**
   a. Did the director use similar techniques across the clips? What are their 'signature moves'?

b. Were there any choices that stood out as particularly impactful in certain scenes? Why?

c. How would you describe the director's overall style in a few words? (Visually focused, dialogue-driven, subtle, flashy, etc.)

Extension:

♦ Consider the thematic concerns of the clips. Try and explain how the director's choices support or reinforce a theme from the text.

♦ Choose two directors working in the same genre. Analyse a scene from each and note down how their stylistic choices support or challenge the genre.

CHAPTER 6

Acting and performance

Acting is the art of portraying characters in a story, a vital element that brings a film to life. It's through the actors' performances that the narrative becomes relatable and emotionally impactful. In this chapter, we'll explore the concept of acting in film and discuss the importance of performance in contributing to the film's overall effect.

Methods and styles of acting

There are various methods and styles of acting, each with its own approach to portraying the character. Method acting involves deeply immersing oneself in the character. Classical acting focuses on a more technical and scripted approach. Aside from these, there are several other methods and styles that actors draw on to connect with and portray their characters:

- **Stanislavski's method** involves drawing upon emotional memories and past experiences to connect automatically with a character's mindset and feelings.
- **Strasberg's method** acting builds on Stanislavski with a greater focus on immersing oneself psychologically into a role over an extended period of preparation.

- **The Meisner technique** emphasises responding instinctively moment to moment rather than planning, using repetitive exercises to ingrain natural reactions.
- **Classical acting** focuses more on external techniques like voice, movement and precisely reacting dialogue rather than mining internal psychology.

Well-known actors associated with each style include Marlon Brando and Daniel Day-Lewis (method); Anthony Hopkins and Cate Blanchett (classical); and Robert De Niro (Stanislavki). Directors often guide actors towards adopting methods suitable to the film's style.

Analysing performance

An important aspect of your film analysis is assessing the quality and impact of an actor's performance. This involves examining how actors convey their character's emotions, intentions and evolution throughout the film. Some important aspects to consider include facial expressions, body language, voice and chemistry with other actors.

Analysing emotional authenticity

- Does the actor effectively and convincingly convey complex emotions like grief, joy, anger, etc., through facial expressions, gestures and body language?
- Do emotional shifts feel earned and genuine – or abrupt/unmotivated?
- Note any moments that feel exaggerated versus subtler, more naturalistic acting choices.

Interpreting character motivations

- What implicit intentions, desires or fears do the actor's choices reveal about the character?
- How do those underlying motivations explain and enrich behaviours and dialogue?

Assessing chemistry and interactions

- Do exchanges between actors have chemistry? Or do they fail to connect?
- For villains/antagonists – does the actor create an intriguing, complex threat?
- When looking at comic relief characters, consider if they're actually humorous. Are their comic moments precisely timed? Do comedic actors bounce off one another smoothly?

Evaluating performative range

- Does the actor display impressive range by transforming themselves physically, emotionally and behaviourally to inhabit contrasting roles?
- Do the actor's choices adjust appropriately to shifting contexts: public versus private persona, younger versus older self?

The role of casting in film

Casting directors select actors who they think will best embody, and compellingly portray, key characters. They play an important role through the choices they make, ensuring that the audience can suspend their disbelief.

Casting directors may need to consider the following scenarios:

- Typecasting has advantages in repeatedly casting actors whose existing gravitas and/or likeability serves a recurring type of role. However, it can also lead to one-note performances or limitations if an actor seeks more variety.

- Casting child actors comes with additional considerations around guarding their welfare on set.

- Authentic casting of minority actors from marginalised groups enables a more empowering insightful portrayal, instead of risking cultural appropriation through whitewashing or stereotypes.

Activity: Performance analysis

Objective:

- Develop an understanding of how acting techniques shape a character's portrayal.
- Practise analysing the elements of acting performance.
- Consider how the actor's choices impact the audience's experience of the film.

Instructions:

1. **Scene selection:** Choose a scene from the film you're studying; a scene where there is a performance that drives it. This could be:

    a. A monologue or confrontation

    b. A scene where a character undergoes a shift in emotion and reveals a secret

    c. A nuanced performance where much is conveyed non-verbally

2. **Viewing:** Watch the scene once without any focus on analysis; just enjoy the performance.

3. **Repeat viewing:** Watch the scene again, this time taking note of the actor's performance. Consider things like:

    a. Body language, posture, gestures, facial expressions

    b. Tone, volume, pitch, pace, accents

    c. How does the actor convey shifts in the character's inner state?

    d. If interacting with others, how does the performance play off the other actors?

4. **Analysis and discussion:**

    a. How did the actor's choices make the character believable and compelling?

    b. Did the performance enhance a theme or mood present in the scene?

    c. Were there specific moments of the performance that were especially impactful?

Extension:

- Find interviews with the actors where they discuss their preparation for the role or insights into the acting process. How does this help with understanding the text?

- Watch the film with the director's commentary on. Do they discuss the choices they made with the actors? How does that help with analysing their performance?

CHAPTER 7

Sound and music in films

Sound is a fundamental component of filmmaking, playing an important role in shaping the audience's experience. It involves more than just dialogue; it encompasses music, sound effects and silence, with each element contributing to the film's atmosphere and storytelling. This chapter explores the various elements of sound in film, explaining their purpose and how they enhance the cinematic experience.

The importance of sound design

Sound design is the process of creating the auditory elements of a film. It involves carefully crafting the soundscape to support the narrative, establish the mood and immerse the viewer in the film's world. Here, we explore the components of sound design, including ambient sound, sound effects and foley art. We'll also look at how sound design can influence the perception of a scene.

Sound design involves carefully crafting a film's soundscape to create immersion, convey emotion and complement the visuals. This requires manipulating and mixing various elements:

- Ambient background sounds like weather, city traffic and local wildlife help establish an authentic sense of place and atmosphere.

- Sound effects punctuate important actions like door slams, breaking glass or machines. Foley artists use props to create exaggerated sound effects, enhancing the film's realism.
- Audio perspective, echoes and muffling create perceptions of characters' distance, settings' scale and offscreen events.
- Automatic dialogue replacement (ADR) is used to fix lines that were recorded imperfectly on set.
- Sound mixing balances the volumes of all the audio tracks into a unified soundscape.
- Audio motifs tie to visual motifs, evolving to reflect the characters' evolution.

Skilled sound design enhances the viewer's emotional experience – amplifying tension, sadness or joy; all the emotions that are tied to the narrative. It can direct audience attention, imply offscreen events and trigger memories through familiar sounds.

Types of film sound: Diegetic and non-diegetic

Understanding the difference between diegetic and non-diegetic sound is essential for your film analysis. Diegetic sounds are those that exist in the film's world – the sounds that characters respond to: a phone ringing, a doorbell, a siren. Non-diegetic sounds, like a film's score or a narrator's voiceover, are not part of the film's reality. They exist outside the frame. Non-diegetic sounds are added for the audience's benefit.

Diegetic and non-diegetic sounds interact in interesting ways. The loud screams of a victim may pierce the non-diegetic backdrop, bringing the audience violently into the scene. A character's emotions, conveyed through the actor's facial expressions, can synchronise with the rise and fall of non-diegetic music. The volume of a lively party's diegetic jazz band may dampen to focus attention on a meaningful glance between characters.

The role of music and score

Music in film serves various purposes, from setting the tone of a scene to evoking specific emotions in the audience. A well-composed score can become a character in the film. The score shapes the film's narrative and adds depth to its emotional arc. Let's explore the role of composers, the process of creating a film's score, and how music is used to complement and enhance the visual storytelling. I've also added some suggestions for iconic film scores to listen to while you write your film analysis.

Film scores use instruments, melodies and song choices to shape emotions, characterise onscreen personas and underscore the film's themes. Composers design identifiable motifs that evolve in sync with a character's trajectory. Minor string instruments heighten sorrow in tragic twists while thunderous brass amplify climactic heroism. Exploring how the musical elements weave with the narrative will deepen your analysis and your appreciation of the film's artistry.

Source music coming from a character's stereos or live bands performing within the film's world provides insights into their personalities and environment. The excessively loud heavy metal blaring in a rebellious teen's bedroom may indicate their anger. A jazz standard wafting in a 1940s New Orleans bar transports the audience into a different time and place through the era-specific sound.

Scores to listen to while you write

Composer	Notable scores
Bernard Herrmann	*Psycho*; *Vertigo*; *Taxi Driver*
Ennio Morricone	*The Good, the Bad and the Ugly*; *Once Upon a Time in the West*; *The Untouchables*
John Williams	*Jaws*; *Star Wars* films; *Indiana Jones* films; *Jurassic Park*
Vangelis	*Chariots of Fire*; *Blade Runner*
Howard Shore	*The Lord of the Rings* trilogy
James Horner	*Titanic*; *Braveheart*; *Avatar*; *Star Trek II* and *III*
Jerry Goldsmith	*Chinatown*; *Mulan Alien*; *Star Trek* films; *Poltergeist*
Hans Zimmer	*The Lion King*; *The Dark Knight*; *Inception*; *Gladiator*

Analysing sound

We now know that sound in film is a vital element. Imagine a film without sound, music or sound effects – DULL! Here are some ways to go about analysing and writing about sound in film. This will be important for completing the analysis of the film you're studying.

Key sequence deep dives:
- Break down scenes to identify the use of dialogue, foley, score and ambient sounds. For example, how does the subtle sound of traffic enhance a tense conversation?
- Examine how sound effects like a sudden screech or distant gunshot foreshadow events or elevate the drama.
- Identify repeating sounds or motifs. Does a specific melody accompany a character, indicating their presence or emotional state?

Character and themes:
- Consider how specific instruments or musical styles are associated with characters. For instance, a solo piano piece might underscore the loneliness of an antihero.
- Explore how relationships are characterised by sounds or songs, enhancing the narrative depth.
- Consider how the score or selected songs emphasise the film's key themes, reinforcing the narrative.

Emotional resonance:
- Explore how music and sound can convey emotions, even without visuals. Make your screen black and listen to the dialogue and the music working together to make you feel something.
- Compare scenes with and without sound to understand its effect on emotional resonance. Mute the TV and note your reactions.

♦ Evaluate how sound, like laugh tracks, influences audience responses. Is that character actually funny, or does the sound of other people laughing make you/the audience laugh?

Stuck with starting your essay? These may help:

1. The use of [specific sound element: ambient noise, score] in this scene effectively [achieves a goal: builds tension, sets the mood] by…

2. In [film title], the director's choice to [include or omit a specific sound] during [specific scene or moment] serves to [explain impact].

3. The recurring motif of [specific sound or type of music] throughout the film parallels [a character or theme's] development by…

4. The contrast between [different types of sound] in [scene or sequence] effectively [creates a specific effect or feeling], which contributes to…

5. The sound design in [specific scene or sequence] plays an important role in [a narrative function: advancing the plot, revealing character], especially when…

Activity: Soundscape detective

Objectives:

- Develop an awareness of how different sound elements work together to create a scene's atmosphere.
- Practise identifying diegetic versus non-diegetic sounds.
- Analyse how sound choices impact the audience's experience.

Instructions:

1. **Scene selection:** Select a scene from the film you're studying where sound plays a significant part. This could be something like:

   a. A suspenseful scene where sound helps to build the tension

   b. A scene with a striking musical score

   c. A scene with lots of contrasting sound elements (nature sounds, dialogue, etc.)

2. **Viewing:** Play the scene focusing only on the sound. It may help to close your eyes and look away from the screen.

3. **Repeat viewing:** Watch the scene again, this time focusing on some of the key sound elements, things like:

   a. Diegetic sound: List all the sounds that seem to exist within the world of the scene.

   b. Non-diegetic sound: List sounds that are added for the audience's experience (music, etc.).

   c. Mood/atmosphere: What feelings or impressions does the soundscape create?

   d. Notable moments: Were there any sound effects or musical shifts that stood out?

4. **Analysis and discussion:**
    a. Were you surprised by any sounds being diegetic/non-diegetic? How did this impact your understanding of the scene?
    b. How do the sound choices contribute to the overall mood and storytelling?
    c. Did the visuals change the way you interpreted the soundscape?

Extension:

- If you have access to editing software, play around with editing, removing or altering the sound. Add your own effects and music. How does this alter your perception of the film?

CHAPTER 8

Editing and post-production

Editing is the process of selecting and arranging the various shots of a film into a coherent sequence. This chapter will explore the critical role of editing in filmmaking, which often goes unnoticed, but significantly impacts the narrative flow, pacing and overall structure of the film. Remember: Everything you watch is constructed. Editing and post-production are the final parts of that construction.

Foundations of film editing

Here are some definitions of some of the foundations of film editing: continuity editing, rhythm and pacing.

Continuity editing
- Ensures logical coherence in storytelling.
- Creates an uninterrupted narrative flow.

Rhythm
- Relates to the timing and duration of shots.
- Contributes to the pacing of the film, impacting the audience's engagement.

Pacing
- The tempo at which the narrative unfolds.
- Editing ensures a balance between tension, excitement and quieter, reflective moments.

Visual effects and CGI

Visual effects and computer-generated imagery (CGI) have transformed modern filmmaking. In this section, we'll look at how visual effects and CGI enhance storytelling by creating engaging and fantastical elements, and by enhancing and expanding settings.

Pioneering visual effects studios like Industrial Light & Magic and Wētā Workshop employ a range of specialised teams to create and craft the director's vision. Visual effects supervisors carefully plan out the required assets, sequences and workflows of all visual effects shots. Teams of people, sometimes situated across the globe (Wētā Workshop is in New Zealand) collaborate on design, animation, coding and composition.

Photoreal CGI, which simulates physics, textures and cinematography identical to live footage, remains challenging. We've all seen a dodgy bit of CGI show up in films. Poor rendering can make environments feel artificial and fake, which impacts the audience's engagement with the film. Because of this, there has been a growing reliance on virtual production methods using real-time game engine previews and LED walls. This merges the practical and digital crafts of filmmaking. Such innovations have also allowed for deceased actors to be resurrected digitally. This isn't without controversy, as was seen in *Rogue One*'s resurrection of Peter Cushing, who played Grand Moff Tarkin in the original *Star Wars*.

Film-editing techniques

We've already covered the basics of film editing, but there are a range of other techniques that you may want to focus on in your analysis to give it depth and nuance. Here are some other things to look for in the film you're studying:

Technique	Explanation	Image/representation
Match on action	Involves cutting from one shot to another while maintaining continuity of action.	
Eye trace	Editors consider the natural movement of the viewer's eye and edit in a way that makes it easy to follow the action.	
Cross-cutting	Involves cutting between two or more scenes that are happening simultaneously.	

Technique	Explanation	Image/representation
Cutaway	A cutaway is a shot that briefly interrupts a continuously filmed action by inserting another related shot, and then returns to the original shot.	
Juxtaposition	Placing two contrasting shots next to each other can create a new meaning or highlight a particular idea or theme.	
Graphic match	Involves cutting between shots that visually complement each other in terms of shape, colour and composition.	
Sound bridge	A technique where the sound from the following scene starts before the visual cut, or the sound from the current scene continues into the next.	

Technique	Explanation	Image/representation
L-cut and J-cut	Editing techniques where the audio and video are cut asynchronously. In an L-cut, the audio from the next scene starts before the visual transition; in a J-cut, the audio from the current scene continues into the next scene.	

Strategies for analysing film editing

Analysing film editing requires an understanding of how the sequencing and combination of shots contribute to the overall storytelling and emotional resonance of the film. Here are some things to look at, which may help you while analysing the editing of your film:

1. **Observing rhythm and pace:** Focus on how the rhythm, dictated by the length and arrangement of shots, impacts the narrative flow and pacing of the film. Consider how fast and slow edits impact the tension and release within scenes, and how this pacing aligns with the film's overall mood and tone.

2. **Identifying editing techniques:** Focus on specific editing techniques, such as jump cuts, cross-cutting, match cuts and fades. Consider how these techniques serve the narrative, whether they are used to create continuity, build suspense, establish relationships or enhance storytelling.

3. **Contributing to the narrative:** How do the editing choices contribute to the development of the plot? Consider how the structure of scenes and the order of events provide clarity or

deliberately disorient the viewer. How does this influence the understanding of the story?

4. **Enhancing themes:** Does the editing underscore or highlight the film's themes? Analyse whether the editing style complements or detracts from the film's content, such as using erratic cuts to reflect a character's mental state, or smooth transitions to evoke a sense of harmony.

5. **Character development:** Examine how the editing choices impact the development of key characters. Notice how certain characters are framed and how their screen time and interactions with other characters are presented. How does this contribute to the audience's perception of them?

6. **Visual and audio elements:** Consider how the visual and audio elements of the film work together. Pay attention to how sound, L-cuts and J-cuts are used to create a seamless audio-visual experience. How does this combination influence the audience's emotional response?

7. **Impact on viewer engagement:** Does the editing engage or alienate the viewer? Consider whether the editing keeps the audience invested in the narrative and characters, or whether it challenges them to piece together the story themselves.

Activity: Editing experiment

Objectives:

- Develop an understanding of how editing techniques shape a scene's meaning and mood.
- Practise the basic principles of film editing (even if it's just with simple software).
- Gain an appreciation of the editor's role in filmmaking.

Instructions:

1. **Editing technique selection:** Focus on two or three editing techniques (for example, cross-cutting, jump cuts, match on action).
2. **Filming:** Film a short scene. The footage should be easy enough to manipulate, even if it's just a few shots of a conversation or an object being moved.
3. **Multiple versions:** Create multiple versions of the same scene using different techniques. For example:
   a. Cross-cutting: Edit the scene to switch back and forth between two parallel actions.
   b. Jump cuts: Create a disjointed effect by removing frames within a single shot.
   c. Match on action: Emphasise smooth continuity by cutting on the flow of an action.
4. **Analysis and discussion:**
   a. How did the techniques dramatically change the tone and pacing of your scene?
   b. Which technique was most effective in conveying a specific mood or idea?

c. Did any edits make the scene confusing or disorienting for the viewer?

Extension:

♦ After editing, remove the original sound. Find sound effects and music to add a completely different mood to your scene.

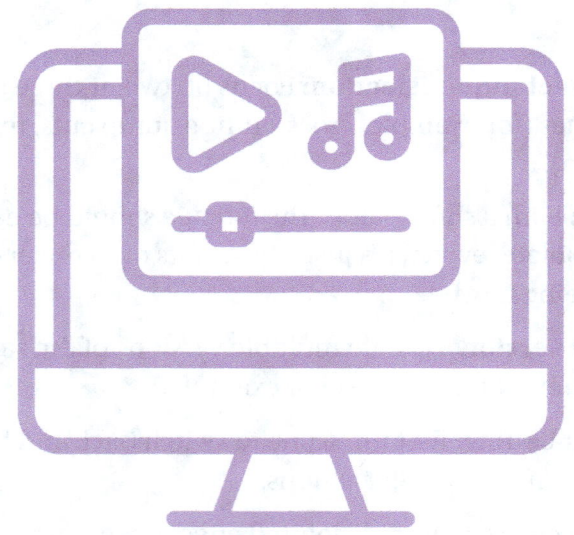

CHAPTER 9

Film criticism and analysis

Film criticism, much like literary criticism, is the art of analysing and evaluating cinema through various lenses, which yields various interpretations. In this chapter, we'll cover the basics of film criticism. Film criticism goes beyond personal opinions; it involves a thoughtful analysis of the elements of filmmaking, such as narrative, themes, cinematography, editing, sound and acting/performance.

Evolution of film criticism

Film criticism traces its origins to the early 20th century when cinema began evolving into a distinct storytelling and artistic form. Silent films inspired commentary on this new medium's storytelling merits, and its comparisons to live theatre. The advent of sound, and the growth of 'talkies' and of Hollywood itself, stimulated even more interest. By the 1950s, film criticism gained legitimacy through major publications like *Cahiers du Cinéma*. Critics interpreted films through various lenses like auteur theory and genre studies, while also judging films on technical qualities and entertainment values.

Approaches to film analysis

Analysts evaluate films from various critical perspectives, much like literary analysis. These critical perspectives emphasise different aspects of the film. Here are some of the main approaches to film criticism, and some things to look for as you review your film through these lenses:

Approach	Explanation	What to look for
Formalist	Focuses on the form and structure of the film, including cinematography, editing, sound and narrative techniques.	Look at how the film's style contributes to its meaning. Consider the use of visual and sound elements, and narrative construction.
Realist	Examines how the film portrays reality, emphasising authenticity, plausibility and naturalism in its presentation.	Observe the depiction of real-world scenarios, the plausibility of characters and settings, and the use of naturalistic techniques.
Auteur	Centres on the director's personal influence on the film, highlighting their individual style and thematic concerns.	Identify the director's signature styles, recurring themes and how their personal vision shapes the film.
Genre	Analyses how a film adheres to, or challenges, genre conventions, including themes, setting and character types.	Focus on the film's alignment with genre norms, use of tropes and any deviations from these.

Approach	Explanation	What to look for
Psychoanalytical	Delves into the psychological aspects of the film, often exploring subconscious, motivations, desires and fears.	Look for symbolic imagery, character motivations and elements that may represent psychological theories or concepts.
Historical	Examines the film in its historical context and how it reflects or reacts to the period in which it was made.	Assess the film's representation of historical events, accuracy and how it reflects the social and cultural contexts of its time.
Feminist	Explores the representation of gender themes, focusing on how the film portrays women and confronts gender norms.	Focus on character dynamics, gender roles, the representation of women, and themes related to gender and feminism.
Ideological	Examines the film's underlying social and political messages, exploring how it portrays social issues and ideologies.	Consider how the film portrays political, social and economic issues, and the film's commentary on these subjects.

Writing film reviews

Writing a film review is a practical application of film criticism. It involves summarising the film's content, analysing its components and providing an informed opinion. Effective reviews balance subjective impressions with objective analysis. A well-written review should address key elements like plot, acting performances, themes, cinematography and editing to provide readers with a deeper insight into the film.

Here are some things to consider if you're going to write a review of your film – this is often a good thing to do before you begin your film analysis:

- **The plot:** When summarising the plot, focus on key narrative arcs without getting into scene-by-scene details. Pay attention to pivotal moments that shape the characters' journeys.

- **Acting:** Analyse the quality of the acting performances, including the actors' abilities to effectively convey emotions and develop believable characters.

- **Themes:** Examine the major themes of the film. What key messages or social commentaries does the movie convey? Observe how techniques like symbolism and character motivation help to develop these themes.

- **Cinematography:** Evaluate the cinematography, including shots, movement, angles and lighting. Consider how this works to establish the mood and tone of the film.

- **Editing:** Assess the film's editing, taking into consideration the pacing, the transitions and the sequencing of shots. Comment on how editing choices have shaped the narrative and the viewing experience.

The role of the critic

The role of the film critic is to provide insightful and informed analyses of films. Critics helps audiences understand and appreciate the nuances of cinema and visual storytelling. They play an important part in shaping the audience's perception and discussion about films.

While offering judgements on quality, the film critic's role involves more than a simple thumbs-up or down review. Serious critics watch movies with an analytical eye, considering directorial and creative decisions, subtexts and technical precision. Their commentaries merge personal opinions with informed analyses. On top of this, critics place films in their historical and social contexts.

If you're stuck with your film analysis, consider accessing some reviews and critiques of your film to help you get started and to give you some food for thought.

Activity: The critic's lens

Objective:

- Develop an understanding of how different critical approaches shape interpretations of the same film.
- Practise applying critical lenses to film analysis.
- Explore the subjective nature of film criticism.

Instructions:

1. **Critical approach selection:** Select a critical approach that intrigues you (formalist, feminist, historical, etc.).
2. **Analysis:** Using the film you're studying, or one of your own choice, analyse it through your chosen lens.
3. **Viewing:** Watch the film, taking detailed notes specifically focused on elements relevant to your chosen lens. Remember to:
   a. Cite specific scenes, dialogue or techniques as evidence.
   b. Consider how your chosen lens influences your interpretation of seemingly neutral elements.
4. **Review and reflection:**
   a. Mini review: Write a two or three paragraph review of the film through your critical lens, arguing your interpretation.
   b. Reflection: Write a short paragraph on how your chosen lens changed your viewing and understanding of the film.

Extension:

- Rewatch the film with a different critical lens. Write a short comparison of your two analyses.
- If you chose the auteur lens, do some research on the director's other films. Do your findings support your auteurist analysis?

CHAPTER 10

Writing an analytical essay on film

Writing an analytical essay on film is an exercise in critical thinking and interpretation. This chapter will bring all the other chapters together and take you through the structure and purpose of a film analysis essay. This requires more than just summarising the plot; it requires an exploration of the film's themes, techniques and impact. Your goal is to craft an insightful argument about the film, supported by evidence and analysis.

Understanding the analytical essay

The structure of an analytical essay typically involves an introduction, body paragraphs and a conclusion. Here's a roadmap of what your essay should look like:

Introduction

- **Purpose:** The introduction sets the stage for your essay. It should grab the reader/assessor's attention and provide them with a roadmap of what to expect.

- **Components:**
  - Main contention: Start with your main contention. This is a concise statement that presents the main argument or perspective of your essay. It should be specific and debatable, and it should answer the essay topic. Your main contention will form the basis of the arguments that you develop in your body paragraphs.
  - Background information: Give a brief overview of the film. This might include title, director and year of release. Providing contextual or historical details might also be beneficial. Don't go overboard, though; your assessors know the texts they assign inside out.

Body paragraphs

- **Purpose:** This is where you will develop your analysis, supporting your main contention with evidence and examples from the film.

♦ **Structure:**

What (topic)	
A sentence that states what feature of the film (a scene, character development, technique, theme) you will discuss.	Example: 'One of the film's most important scenes is when...'

⬇

How (analysis and evidence)	
Detailed descriptions and examples from the film to illustrate the element you're discussing. This could include quotes, shots, sounds and lighting.	Example: 'The director uses close-up shots and dim lighting in this scene to...'

⬇

Why (explanation and interpretation)	
Analyse the implication of this element. Discuss how it contributes to the film's themes, audience's understanding or societal/cultural values.	Example: 'This technique is effective in conveying the character's isolation because...'

⬇

So (connection to main contention)	
End the paragraph by linking the discussion back to your main argument, reinforcing how this element contributes to your interpretation of the film as a whole.	End the paragraph by linking the discussion back to your main argument, reinforcing how this element contributes to your interpretation of the film as a whole.

English and Media Studies assessors love fresh thinking and individual interpretation. They also like individual writing. Don't be scared to change up this structure as your essay comes together: How, What, Why, So; So, What, Why, How. This will keep your writing fresh and engaging – and push it up the marking scale!

Conclusion

- **Purpose:** The conclusion provides closure to your essay, reinforcing your main arguments and leaving your reader/assessor something to ponder.

- **Components:**
  - Restate your main contention, but in different words. This should reflect the insights and arguments you've made in your essay.

  - Summarise the main points of your essay. Don't introduce new information, just remind your assessor that you know what you're talking about.

  - End with a final thought or insight into the text.

Formulating a main contention

To successfully complete your film analysis essay, you need to provide a strong central point. This will anchor your essay. The main contention is more than just a summary of the film's plot; it's a clear and debatable argument that serves as the foundation of your entire analysis. It should offer a unique perspective or insight into the film, showcasing your deep and nuanced analytical mind at work.

Characteristics of a main contention

1. **Clarity:** Your contention should be clearly stated, leaving nobody guessing about what you're trying to argue in your essay. It should be specific enough to provide a clear direction for your analysis.

2. **Arguable:** A good main contention is not a statement of fact, but rather an argument that others could potentially dispute. This allows for a more engaging and thought-provoking analysis.

3. **Insightful:** Go beyond the obvious or superficial aspects of the film. A strong contention often delves into deeper themes, stylistic choices, minor characters or the cultural and social implications of the film.

4. **Focused:** While it should be insightful, it also needs to be focused and manageable. A broad contention can lead to a scattered analysis.

Steps to formulating your main contention

1. **Reflect on the film:** Think about what aspects of the film left the most significant impression on you. Was it the narrative structure, the visual style, the themes and ideas or the character development?

2. **Identify a focus:** Based on your reflection, choose a specific focus for your analysis. This could be an examination of the film's handling of a particular theme, its use of cinematography or how it challenges social norms.
3. **Develop an argument:** Transform your observations into an arguable statement. For example, instead of stating, 'The film uses flashbacks a lot', you might argue, 'The film's use of non-linear storytelling through flashbacks mirrors the protagonist's fragmented memory.'
4. **Make it supportable:** Make sure that your contention can be supported with evidence from the film. It should be something you can back up through details, analysis and examples.

Here are five sentence starters that will help you introduce your essay's main contention:

1. At the core of [film title] lies the exploration of [theme/idea], as the film uses [specific element] to explore the complexities of [subject].
2. Through its [specific aspect: narrative style, visual effects], [film title] challenges conventional perceptions of [genre/theme/idea], redefining the audience's understanding of [concept].
3. [Film title] transcends the typical boundaries of its genre by [specific action: complex narrative, cinematography, colour], offering a fresh perspective on [theme/idea].
4. The director's use of [specific technique/approach] in [film title] not only enhances the storytelling, but also serves as a critical commentary on [social/cultural theme], revealing deeper layers of meaning.
5. [Film title] stands out for its [character development, visual style], which plays an important role in illustrating the film's underlying message about [theme/idea].

Incorporating techniques

Your essay should demonstrate an understanding of film techniques and how they contribute to the meaning of the film you're studying. Discuss elements like narrative structure, editing style, use of sound and music, and cinematography, and how they contribute to the film's overall effect. Here are some things to keep in mind when writing about film techniques in your essay:

1. **Use detailed observations:** Make detailed observations of the film's technical aspects. Note down specific scenes (using timestamps will mean you can come back to it later as well) where techniques like lighting, editing or sound play an important part in the storytelling.

2. **Provide context:** When discussing a technique, provide the context within the film. Describe the scene briefly before diving into your analysis. This will help your reader/assessor understand the significance of the technique you're discussing.

3. **Analyse the effect:** Consider how the technique influences the audience's perception or emotion. How does it enhance the storytelling?

4. **Link techniques to themes:** Make connections between the technical aspects and the film's larger themes. Discuss how the cinematography, sound and editing choices reflect or underscore the film's message.

5. **Talk the talk:** Familiarise yourself with and use the specific language of film in your essay. This will not only demonstrate your vast knowledge of film, but will also allow for a precise analysis.

6. **Quotes:** If relevant, incorporate quotes from the directors, cinematographers or film critics that may help shed light on the intention behind certain techniques.

Using examples effectively

Purpose of examples

- Examples are the backdrop of your analysis. They're important for illustrating your points, making your analysis more compelling.

How to choose examples

- Select scenes, dialogue or cinematic techniques that directly relate to your main contention/argument.
- Look for moments in the film that are important for its narrative, themes or emotional impact.

Describing examples

- When describing examples, include enough detail to paint a clear picture for your reader/assessor.
- Mention the context, the characters involved, specific camera angles, lighting and sound, and how these contribute to the scene's overall effect.

Analysing examples

- After describing the example, analyse it.
- Explain why this example is significant and how it supports your main contention.
- Discuss the filmmaker's possible intention and the effect on the audience.

Editing and proofreading

Editing and proofreading your essay are important steps in the writing process. We often overlook them, but after all your hard work, you don't want your main argument to be diluted because you misspelled a few words. At this final stage, here are some things to consider:

- **Logical flow:** Review your essay to make sure that it progresses logically from one point to the next. Make sure your paragraphs transition smoothly from one to the next.
- **Paragraph structure:** Double-check each paragraph to make sure you've ticked off the What, How, Why, So elements.
- **Support and evidence:** Ensure that for every example, technique and character, you have supported all your points with appropriate evidence from the film.
- **Main contention and argument:** Make sure that the entire essay remains focused on supporting your main contention. Each paragraph should contribute to building your overall argument.

When you've made sure all the big-picture things are taken care of, zero in on the small things: the grammar, spelling and punctuation.

  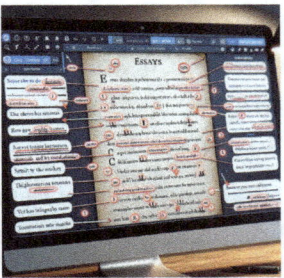

Grammar
- Use a grammar-checking tool as a first step.
- Read your essay carefully, paying close attention to common issues like subject-verb agreement, proper tense and sentence structure.

Spelling
- Use your word processor's spell-checking software; these can catch most spelling errors.
- Don't just rely on your word processor, though; go over your entire essay to look for words that are spelled correctly but are in the wrong context (their versus there, etc.).

Punctuation
- Ensure proper use of commas, full stops, semicolons and other punctuation.

Here are some other things to think about when editing and proofreading your essay:

- **Read aloud:** Reading your essay out loud can help you catch errors or weird phrasing that you might miss when reading silently.

- **Peer review:** If possible, have a friend review your essay. Fresh eyes can often help with catching mistakes that you've overlooked. They can also provide feedback on your essay.

- **Take a break:** If time allows, step away from your essay for a day or two before editing and proofreading. This can help you approach your work with a fresh perspective, making it easier to find areas for improvement.

Concluding thoughts

And that concludes this study in film analysis and film writing. I hope you found it useful and you're now confident in smashing your assessments! While this is important, you should also remember that the joy of cinema lies not only in dissecting its elements, but also in the simple pleasure of immersing yourself in a captivating story.

For those planning on further study of film, continue to develop your analytical skills, but never forget to appreciate the magic of the movies. Whether you're writing an essay, preparing for an exam or simply watching a film for fun, always approach it with a sense of wonder and appreciation. After all, a lot of people worked a lot of hours to get that film to your living room. Just look at all the names in the end credits!

www.ingramcontent.com/pod-product-compliance
Lightning Source LLC
Chambersburg PA
CBHW070323120526
44590CB00017B/2798